HIGH FIRE DANGER

*poems in response to
the Black Summer bushfires
2019 – 2020*

© Emma Trenorden   2024

All rights reserved. Except for appropriate use in a book review, no part of this publication may be reproduced, stored in a retrieval system, or transmitted in any form or by any means, without the prior permission of the publisher, or in the case of photocopying or reprographic copying, a licence from the Copyright Agency of Australia.

High Fire Danger

ISBN 9780645797763

Walleah Press
South Launceston
Tasmania, Australia 7249

www.walleahpress.com.au

ralph.wessman@walleahpress.com.au

HIGH FIRE DANGER

By Emma Trenorden

For Asher and Cole

CONTENTS

I cinder	1
rear-view mirror	3
in one long inhale	4
sideways	6
explode	7
winnow	8
recalibrate	10
as I close my eyes	12
sidelined	13
beyond	14
II smoke	15
thunderhead	17
burn and blister	18
the weight	20
urgent comfort	21
cool bathroom tiles	22
coastline cradle	25
amphibious	26
alight	27
unlikely companions	28
we spark and we burn	29
fleeting revelations	30

III coal	31
left behind	33
unburied	34
nest	35
icy release	36
husk	38
the careless wind	40
sizzling hot highway	41
tarnished	42
where the creeks run cooler	44
buoyant turning	46
IV ash	47
a burnt forest	49
afterwards	50
sift	52
waves	53
at dusk	54
new skin	56
scars	57
spears	58
new map	59
Author's bio	62
Notes	62
Acknowledgements	63

I

cinder

rear-view mirror

click
fasten my seatbelt
snatch a look in the rear-view mirror
red geraniums spill over the retainer wall
a tangle of pink bougainvillea needs pruning
I lurch from the car
stumble back up
the gravel driveway

scraps of ash float through the orange air

click
I snap a photo on my phone
click click
back to the car
slam the door
seatbelt back on
release the handbrake
look in the mirror one last time

a whole home captured

in one

fleeting

frame

in one long inhale

Ever wonder what it feels like to be on the inside of a snow dome,
picked up and shaken until the sky falls down?
Not a festive scene with delicate snowflakes that parachute tenderly,
instead, the world burns from the inside out, blows blustery.

Amid the scratchy noise I look across to our neighbour's house,
see power lines exposed and eucalypts windblown.
As I reach for the last sheet on the line,
I feel a drop in the wind, the clatter falls silent,
and in the quiet I can almost hear
the sound of our neighbourhood breathing

in

and out

like a familiar chorus, practised in singing,
many bodies inhale and exhale as one.
I sense the collective inhalation
the filling of our lungs with air
and then the waiting.

Just yesterday I was out on the water, being pulled out to sea
before rushing back in with the wave.
But this wave, rising now, is a monstrous mouth of smoke and ash
coming our way, ominously, we do not see the sparks nor flames,
but hear them in a static buzzing, just out of reach,
behind the menacing curtain of haze.

Then a plane drops a load of fire retardant
and a stream of cloud

spills

from the sky

it's raining

from the mechanical bird
dousing patches to fight the growing monster
while I hurry my washing inside.

All of this happens   in   one   long   inhale

with a blood sun sinking into a sea of smoke

while I wait for the neighbourhood chorus

to start breathing,

to start singing,

again.

sideways

out the front of her home
she stands
protective

arms at her side
she looks straight at us
as if about to say
something

hair blowing to one side
tall trees lean in the same
direction

behind her
amidst a golden glow ablaze
he stands on a porch
holding onto
a rail

upright
hands firmly grasping
while all around him
a sky of fire blows
sideways

explode

a gumtree burns from the inside out
across the road leaning

hostile sneezes of cinders explode
hot hungry tongues snacking

ahead we see a winding road
lined with witches' hats, lights blinking

of a fire truck, red and white tape
shouting colours of alarm

I turn to you, unspeaking
how did we get here?

winnow

both of us bicker, our tempers boil,
    we are mid-argument when we see

the solitary kangaroo glide through
    bushland shrouded in a golden haze

so we pull the ute to the side of the road
    leave the engine running

while we scan the scene, I can still hear
    the car stereo, muffled

an all-too familiar tune, but right now
    it plays out of place – these *flame trees*

will blind the weary driver, and there's
    nothing else could set fire to this town

these eucalypts are not yet ablaze
    this woodland is intact, for now,

trees bear the brunt of a torrid gust
    remain poised even as smoke fans and billows

but the kangaroo is no longer seen
    it has left us here, wordless

as the smoke grows thicker by the minute
    tainted air fills my lungs

so I exhale, try to empty it all out
        but it backfires as I breathe back in

and I begin to hear fiery sparks
        flicker in the distance, soft at first,

then the sound grows louder
        you must read the panic in my eyes

so you reach for my arm and lead me back
        to the ute, to the chorus reminding me

of *the flame trees* and *everything within*
        its place, as if I needed reminding

of the colour of the sky aflame
        or the breath of wind in my hair, winnowing

or the taste of burnt earth as it catches
        at the back of my throat, hard to swallow

I'm not sure if the song ends
        before you place your hand on my thigh

and we drive on
        the details of the remaining day

dissipate,
        unimportant

recalibrate

we glimpse a ship slipping through
a sea of orange mist

on shore, a lamp, subdued
attempts to cut through
the fire-lit dimness

I take off my reading glasses
wipe the lens clear
but when I replace them
I find we are still

here,
somewhere between
day and night
like penguins
huddled

on a beach
taking shelter -
is this really real?

with the sun
in the middle of the day
nowhere to be seen
we are

reinterpreting what we mean
by wake
and sleep

as I close my eyes

falling asleep
I see them still

they peer through
an amber daze

questioning eyes
pierce the haze

pleading,
as I drive away

cattle stand in a field
marooned

silently swallowed by a cindery sky
alive and breathing

all encompassing
enclosing

as I close

my

eyes

sidelined

sitting together
we watch the news updates

on screen a helicopter hovers
above a burning woodchip mill
a furore of exhaust wheezes up
and sideways
the angry blaze raging
fuming
inconsolable

meanwhile
a body of water lies adjacent
placid waves lap quietly
calmly caress the mill's stone wall
only metres from the quickening blaze

separated by an immovable wall of stone

together we are –

sidelined

beyond

smoke rises
in a sooty
tower

colossal
climbing
into the sky

ascending
reaching
soaring

at the peripheries
cotton wool stretches to burnt rust
and golden brown, simmering

a hint   of   blue   whispers   on   the   horizon

beyond

if we dare lift our gaze

that

far

II

smoke

thunderhead

high above
a pyrocumulonimbus cloud amasses

a giant filthy grey thunderhead sitting atop
billowing smoke

the beast grows
unrelenting

fuelled

from

beneath

burn and blister

they confront a wall of fire
it radiates
presses at them
spits fire balls
blasts sweltering winds

the fire crew puts themselves between
the fire wall and a family home
they are human flesh
fighting this creature of flame
wing-less but leaping and flying
all the same

the human flesh fighters fight on
they press back
burn and blister
spit back
sweat and swear
blast back
until the fire wall subsides
like a fever breaking
momentarily
before it directs its hostility
elsewhere

the fire crew roll up their hoses
they must keep pushing on
pressing on
to the next
battle front

the weight

a fire fighter holds a hose
heavy above their head
the white sticky spray
bursts out in a horizontal line
covering charcoal surfaces

unyielding

urgent comfort

a mother grabs at her children
urging aboard a helicopter
hair sweeping behind
earplugs in
blankets spilling out of a backpack
a soft toy clutched under a small arm

holding onto

a little

piece

of comfort

cool bathroom tiles

a flash
and the day turns to night
flames leap
and fan out wide

from above,
cinders rain down
in diagonal blustery gusts
while I race to clear a firebreak
set the sprinklers
soak the roof
throw buckets of water on the garden
then retreat

as I hurry through the house
eyes smarting
lungs full of smoke
grab my son's fishbowl
take it with me
to the cool bathroom tiles
blankets wet and ready

outside the air brightens
orange red pink
purple neon burns electric white
as fire sweeps through in a frenzy
incinerating the forest
to monochrome shades
ghostly

inside I lie on my side
watching the fish
White Clouds
I remember asking
Why this name?
the small silver-green fish
I was told by my seven year old
are native to White Cloud Mountain
right now they are clouds of a guided meditation
slowing my breathing
and though I find I cannot move my limbs
I watch their iridescent scales
slip through the water
the orange red flicker of their tails
transfixing

outside the firestorm howls
a guttural sound that fills the sky
in a crescendo
before it blusters by

it skirts the house, the sheds and motorbike
spares the kids trampoline and swing set
left to creak back and forth in its wake

while inside I lie, unmoving
gazing into the fishbowl
my body still pressed

to the
cool
bathroom
tiles

coastline cradle

hundreds of us cluster on a beach
the water in safe reach
we turn our faces beyond a stretch of sand
where forest meets sea

plumes of smoke grey, orange, pink
surge skyward as a rising giant
blanketing the sun
leaving us in shadow
listening to a distant sound
of houses, cars, whole towns
as they shatter, blast, explode

behind us waves shush and cradle
lapping in and out
the coastline stretches like big arms holding

as we become smaller
a flock of sheltering seabirds
craning our necks
to the heavens

we reach for
each other's hands

clinging to
the water's edge

amphibious

navy ships pluck us from beaches
we are strapped into an amphibious vehicle

beside me, a parent and child share a smile
I tuck your photo safely into my breast pocket

glancing back I see

others still on shore
left waiting

into phones
looking

out to sea
staring

alight

you are seated in a Hercules flight deck
windows sweep around front and sides
the military aircraft enveloped
by a translucent golden veil
something out of a sci fi movie
but this is real

below, we hide and take shelter
as waves of rippling smoke
fill an unsettled sky
you are tasked to find your way to us
to deliver supplies
navigating your way
through this fragile skyscape
alight

inside with headphones on
receiving instructions
from screens of green light
you attempt to
to land

unlikely companions

face concealed by helmet and visor
a soldier carries a small black dog
eyes blinking from a blanket
stunned

soldier and dog
unlikely companions
boarding a loud
mechanical
stranger

we spark and we burn

hands on hips
arms crossed
we watch –

a silhouette of bystanders
our shadow forms a union
of our witnessing

big, old trees crackle and snap
yellow flames flicker orange
explode red
defeat coal black

the heat of the flames
permeates our skin
its rage and panic
also in our eyes

as the sky sparks
and the earth burns
we spark
and we burn

fleeting revelations

satellite images show a landmass of sepia tones
an arid land, parched
its ochre hues bleached and overcooked

rivers, arteries of seaweed colour, branch outward
into clusters of deepening green
borne of the land, they distil into the ocean,
imbibed by an expansive sapphire mirror

patches of soft white sprinkle over the interior
graduate to grey blankets
in a wide, smeared, paint stroke sweeping east

glimpses of a seared coastline

burnt seaweed

filter through

our beautiful devastation

revealed in fleeting moments

seen from space

III

coal

left behind

a scorched forest
dumbstruck

bewildered posts
of charred midnight grey

left behind
in a smoky blue film

stripped of any verve
unmoving

unburied

burned animal carcasses
lie along the road

legs in the air
strewn sideways

their disfigured cooked bodies
unburied

nest

the sky dissolves to red

an eerie filter on the world

a fence line rendered no use

a tree abandoned, but one bird's nest

empty

deserted

or perhaps waiting

for a return?

icy release

I've been lying in bed for hours
sunlight slips through the drawn curtains
keeping me from sleep
you decide enough time has passed
before you come to lift me to my feet
gently wrap your arm around my back
place hat on my head, sunglasses over eyes
before we step out into the glaring day

my body recoils from the lingering smell
of fried earth, smoky air
we walk to the end of the street, down the hill
then cut through the laneway to the beach
sea spray spits at us as we approach
and I hold my hat against my head
determined to keep the glaring sun at bay

I make a beeline for the water
for the first time in days
my body seeks something out
hungry for the ocean's cold bite

rubbing my soles into the grain of the sand
I feel for rough rocks, sharp edges of broken shells
the frothy waves trickle over my toes
wash up against my ankles
I want the icy coolness to find its way through my skin
cut deeper still, to inhabit the bones of my toes, feet, legs
so I inch further in, up to my knees
and stay here a while

waves crash against my legs
their chilly slaps releasing some of the heat
burning up inside me for days

after some time I retreat to ankle-deep
and listen for the bubbly fizz
spraying over my toes
before sizzling back out to sea

my feet begin to walk
with an urgency I've not felt for days
my mind still a smoky daze

kickstarted by the cold
my feet find their own way

husk

we return to a home in pieces
scattered piles of corrugated iron

debris ripped, blown around,
as if cardboard

beams of steel that once held up a roof
lie drooped, like melted chocolate in a hot car

my legs give way and I find myself kneeling
pressing down into the chalky ash

beside the gutted house
a stoic mountain gum smoulders

I eye the once smooth shine of its trunk
and wonder at the shape of its roots

reaching down into the ground
into the cool, moist earth

holding water still
in these perilous times

I rise to my feet
a cicada husk clasped in hand

my fingers curl around it
press into the emptiness

and don't let go

the careless wind

along a fire edge thousands of kilometres long
trucks and bulldozers tumble in
unload a tired crew
dressed in high vis
they go to a tree lying sideways
in a circle of orange blaze
cylindrical
flames lick their way through
the tree's interior
carving a central smouldering tunnel

the hiss of embers is interrupted
by the piercing trill of a chainsaw
it slices the log into bite-sized pieces
for someone else to hose it down
while another rakes dirt and ashes

all the work unseen
to smother cinders
lest the careless wind turn -
breathing life into this fire edge
fanning it into a fire wall

from spark
exploding to ravenous flames

on the move
and hunting

sizzling hot highway

a lone koala
at the side of a road
in the middle of a blackened plain
the heat still steams
from the charred tar

paws singed
eyes glazed
she wraps a blanket around
the unmoving animal
cradles it like a baby
to the airconditioned car

big eyes unblinking
as they drive away

slipping along

the sizzling hot

highway

tarnished

as you grow inside me
fires burn across the country

your placenta forms
and I feed you
outside, in our skies
soot absorbs sunlight
heats clouds, sends them rising

a river of smoke high above us
crosses the Tasman
turns the sky a tarnished tangerine
as your little heart starts to beat

you grow organs, limbs,
tiny hands and feet
while plumes pass overhead
tracked by satellites
and troubled scientists

a kick
a wriggle
a hiccup
you press and push outward

the smoky river also turns
along the way drops ash deposits
as it crosses oceans
passes over whole continents
in multiple orbits

then in your final month
your lungs are ready
to come out into the world
to breathe life in
yet I can't help but wonder

where have I led you?

where the creeks run cooler

I mute the TV when I hear footsteps on the stairs
try to shield her from the numbing news
new waves of fires, floods, wars, virus

I lead her back to her room
she asks for a story
The big pink slug!
so I tell her about volcanic eruptions
millions of years ago
that pushed up the earth
carved narrow valleys and steep ridges
chiselled the Sawn Rocks of Mount Kaputar

high above surrounding forests
a Sky Island formed
here it was cooler
rain fell and sometimes a sprinkling of snow
it's here the giant slugs still live today
what colour are they? *Hot pink!*
in the day you won't see them
where could they be?
They hide in the leaves! In the bottoms of trees!

then in the dark they come out
climb the trunks of Snow Gums
hungry, they slide up into the forest canopy
foraging for lichen and moss
on cool wet misty mornings
you'll see hundreds of them
coming back down the trees
before they hide again
their bright pink squishy bodies
finding somewhere cool and dark
and before I finish the story
she's asleep

I don't tell her of the slugs lost to fires
but also that others survived
found shelter in damp rock crevices
as flames swept by

I switch off the bedside lamp
stay for a moment under the soft blanket
wrapped by dark and quiet
I make a promise to bring her back up
to the remnants of ancient volcanoes
back up into the Sky Island
where the creeks run cooler
and in the damp leaf litter
fluorescent pink slugs hide

buoyant turning

thick plumes of white and dirty grey sweep the coastline

puffing from the ground up
frantically climbing
joining
to become a smothering mass
concealing
anything beyond

the neighbouring green sea
lies seemingly still
though waves continue to crash

steadfast
in their buoyant turning

unfaltering
in their returning

in and out
with our breathing

IV

ash

a burnt forest

a burnt forest
akin to a cemetery
with marking posts

a tree stands at the centre
formidable

an outer layer of bark charred black
begins to strip back
peeling
revealing
a soft flush tender new skin
vulnerable

at the base new shoots blossom
like roses sprinkled
at the feet

an offering to the dead

and to

the living

afterwards

afterwards
the silence is deafening
the radiating heat of the inferno
lingering
still ringing
in our ears

it is only when
that heightened drone subsides
that we notice the absence
of the cicadas humming
or the white noise
of small creatures scurrying
across the forest floor
and the wind in the trees whistling
a soundtrack taken for granted
like our breathing

music returns now
slowly, tentatively
intermittently
like the chorus of chirruping crickets
or the fleeting refrain of birds
passing through the stripped forest
then gone again

suddenly an abrupt shouting
of bulldozers and chainsaws
plays out in a ballad of humans returning
to clean up
to clear the slate
to rebuild
to start
again

sift

walking over cushioned soot
crackle crunch hiss
an entire home reduced
to a carpet of black and grey

I want to take off my boots
to feel the heat still in the corpse
and press my feet into
what remains

instead I kneel
scoop a handful of matter
part earth and fire
part wood and metal
the chalky grit
sifts through my fingers
fine particles first
then larger fragments

and blows away

I rub my hands together
see the black under the nails
feel the rough grain
sticking to my skin
like sandpaper rubbing down
my grandfather's old writing desk
smoothing, polishing the wood
now a part of this carpet of ashes

waves

we walk along a beach
feet and paws press into raven flakes of ash
with soft golden sand beneath

you scamper ahead
a shimmer in the water catches my eye
I bend to scoop a handful of sand
the fine blonde particles
adorned with insects
metallic shield bugs iridescent blue green
ladybirds orange and black
some with their wings spread
their brittle shells washed ashore
having drowned as they fled

you come to see what I've found, tail-wagging
I return the insect shells to the sea
then follow your lead
when I lift my gaze I see
the tar stretch onwards
patterns of ebony on gold
shift with the waves washing in
unwavering in their arriving

we keep walking
as seagulls look on
also pondering
this new world

at dusk

I walk up the creek bed to find you
once open-armed, reaching wide and tall
you hosted parties of galahs
raucous green budgies covered your limbs
a hotel with live music every evening
as the sun went down

now lying flat to the ground
you still offer shelter
to the geckos and skinks
and other small creatures
who survived the black days
the lucky and resilient ones
who will return with rain

I take a seat
beside your uprooted trunk
once anchored surely
now ripped sideways
at the base I see charcoal rings
in shades of grey
the concentric lines
quietly speak your age

my hand strokes your outer skin
now cracked, fractured
a gust of wind stings my eyes
with a pungent charred odour
bringing tears
raining down
upon your cracked skin

new skin

charcoal columns lay in disarray
toppled upon powdery ash
covering the earth
in a layer of new skin

clouds creep across the sky
and I awake to an ashen-tinged petrichor
that makes me both smile and weep

staying in bed I listen
to the gentle patter on dirt
surprised to hear the raaaaa
of a spotted-tree frog
as patter turns to drumming
rain slaps the earth
frogs sing along
raa – raa – raa

I pull on my gumboots and step outside
as I squelch and splash in puddles
I spot wombat droppings
and fresh new sprigs
tangerine-coloured leaves
rise up, surround me
some scarlet blood

so alive

in their
sprouting

scars

a close-up of a tree's armour
lines etched into coal
muted grey at the edges
sharper black marks at the interior
of this organic matter
living, breathing, scars
of an inferno

at the centre
in sharp focus
leaves of emerald, peach,
apricot
unapologetic
in their colour

spears

tufts of spiky heads protrude
from cooked stumps

green canes with sharp orange tips

spears clawing out
from the ashen crust

new map

I stop, map in hand,
the fixed lines printed on paper
don't match the terrain I see lying before me
so I angle the map sideways
turn it upside down and around
but no matter the direction I try
I can't seem to reconcile
paper with land

I see no clear path ahead
just a sea of green low-lying shrubs
with little pink stars shimmering
like a night sky's reflection
on dark glassy water

taking a seat on the rocky ground
I draw on my water pack, thirsty
I've been walking a good hour
but it's only now I hear the wind
a murmur of it through the green growth
its cool breeze mixes with the warmer air
raising the hairs on my arms

star-shaped flannel flowers
paint the Blue Mountains pink
covering blackened land unabashedly
only a month ago their seeds lay dormant

these hills kissed black by the flames
and now the flowers flourish, they bloom,
moving with the wind
like floating ballerinas

but even surrounded
by this bold display of life renewed
I can't help but think of others
wiped away
incinerated
The Snowy River Westringia
The Orchid Dupe Wasp

species move across a sliding scale
- vulnerable, threatened, endangered -
inching ever closer to the precipice

The Kangaroo Island Echidna
The New Holland Mouse, Pookilla
The Purple Copper Butterfly
The Golden-Tipped Bat
The Broad-Toothed Rat
The Honey Blue-Eye Fish
The Alpine She-Oak Skink
The Spotted Tree Frog
The Superb Lyrebird
The Bago Leek Orchid
The Granite Leaf-Tailed Gecko
The Red-Browed Treecreeper
The Braidwood Waratah
The Mount Imlay Boronia
The Macleay Valley Pinwheel Snail

I shape their names with my mouth
whisper them aloud
to the shifting breeze
- a prayer, a plead -

to keep them out in the world
beneath rocks
in rivers, creeks,
on land, hiding in hollows of trees
wings taking to the sky, soaring free
let them not be reduced
to names listed in a book
their bones preserved
put on display in a museum
for my children to observe

I return the map to my pack
and rise to my feet
breathing the cool air in deep

with the smell of rain approaching
I lean in

to the flannel flowers
dancing

to a distant horizon
opening

to a cloud covered sky
cicadas humming

Author's bio

Emma Trenorden is a poet, singer-songwriter, and a creative arts therapist living in Mparntwe, Alice Springs.

Emma has had poems published in 'Campfire Satellites: an inland anthology' (New South Books) and the 'Australian Poetry Anthology' (Volume 7, 2019). In her work developing Indigenous literacy resources, she has worked on the publication of educational resources including a book for young adults called 'Tjulpu and Walpa' (NPY Women's Council).

In 2022 she was selected to further develop her debut poetry manuscript, *high fire danger*, through an Arts NT Varuna Writers Fellowship. One of these poems, 'a burnt forest', was Highly Commended in the NT Writers' Centre Poetry Award of the NT Literary Awards. 'afterwards' was published in Issue 16 of *Feral – A Journal of Poetry and Art*. She shares inights into her songwriting at www.storiesfromtheheart.com.

Notes

The poem 'Winnow' (page 8) references the Cold Chisel song 'Flame Trees' from the band's 1984 album 'Twentieth Century', (songwriting credits Steve Prestwich and Don Walker).

Acknowledgements

Emma would like to thank Sue Fielding, Leni Shilton, Barbara Lewis, and Liam Campbell for the feedback, care and encouragement of these poems. Thanks also to Arts NT and the Varuna Writers' House for the residency that supported the development of a few fledgling poems into a manuscript and to Mary Anne Butler whose mentoring as part of that residency encouraged me to explore the artist's path of holding grief and hope in these unsettling times.

www.ingramcontent.com/pod-product-compliance
Lightning Source LLC
Chambersburg PA
CBHW022022290426
44109CB00015B/1271